C000138685

Melancholy

&

Cinnamon

A JOURNEY THROUGH MENTAL HELL

GABRIELLE G.

Cover by Gabrielle G.
Cover Illustration by Zab. C.
Poems and Formatting by Gabrielle G.
Pictures from Exhale by Gabrielle G.

First Printing, 2021
ISBN 978-1-7774882-2-2

Gabrielle G.
PO 40527
Kirkland, QC
H9H 5G8 CANADA
www.authorgabrielleg.com

"I have nature and art and poetry, and if that is not enough, what is enough?"

Vincent van Gogh

BY THE SAME AUTHOR

Poetry Collection

To the man I loved too much

Contemporary Love Stories

Always & Only

Never & Forever

Often & Suddenly

Heartbroken

Forsaken

Untamed

Darling

Trouble

Sweet

Mended

The Secrets We Keep

Follow Gabrielle G. on Amazon to keep up to date with her latest release or visit her website www.authorgabrielleg.com and subscribe to her newsletter.

To my love;
Thank you for holding me, when darkness was all I saw,
For helping me breathe when everything felt raw.
You are the cinnamon of my melancholy,
The true reason why I write poetry...

I Was Made Of Words

I looked in the mirror, trying to find myself
But all I could see was a pile of words
Depicting the blackness I hid behind bookshelves
And the spell I chanted like mourning birds.

So I cried in verses and hurt in rhymes,
Poem after poem trying to heal my pain,
Without believing I'll see another sometimes,
As sadness rushed into every one of my veins.

The storm calmed down on my demons' striate
Thanks to the rhythm of every stanza
And as the sun rose on my heart's riot,
I found in the mirror who I was looking for.

As my mind discovered its own ingenuity
And my soul rose from all its unforeseen shadows,
I wore a shining smile made of poetry
And my eyes feasted on the most beautiful prose.

DETERIORATION

the process of becoming progressively worse.

Invisible

As I hear them talking without me,
All I want to do is disappear
Become as insignificant as my presence in their
conversation
As invisible as the pain they can't see.

Hardship

Tears cloud my mind.
Another day in hell.
Alone and blind,
Rotting in my cell.

Voices screaming at me,
All their condemnation.
Showing I'm unworthy,
Even for depression.

Love spread around,
But never whispered to me.
I fell on the ground,
Can anyone help me?

But no one sees my pain,
No one hears their scream.
The silence sounds the same,
When you lose all esteem.

I Love Tea

Darkness steeps in my heart
Brewing madness in my blood
Slowly poisoned, I fall apart
And my thoughts become mud.

Hide and Seek

I hide in the darkness of my mind
Waiting for nightfall to come
But hoping my muted scream keeps me awake
So I don't fall in the slums of death

Killer

In breathing in light
I choked on my darkness,
And gave up on the fight
Against my sadness.

You were supposed to heal me,
To take me under your wings,
But all you did was destroy me
and clip me with a ring.

Now I cry my demons,
Let the voices insult me.
Who could keep all their reason
When they feel so crazy?

In breathing in light
I choked on my darkness,
Gave up hopes of life
And embraced my own death.

Evening Hope

I wanted a fresh night,
Made of laughter and cherry bites
But I woke to an anxious high
My mind begging for a fight.

The Taste of Depression

Blood
Kiss
Love
Pain
Tears
Salty lips

In the moment, I survive
    Behind a smile hiding lies
    Trying to keep myself alive
    Without tears in my eyes.

In the moment, I love
    A quick instant of hope
    Forgetting all the "should have"
    And the life I can't elope.

In the moment, I am
    Race and sprint of pain
    Screams and anagram
    Of the chain on my brain.

In the moment, I flee
    In a world of expression
    For a moment my poetry
    Soothes my depression.

No one sees my secrets
No one sees my fight
No one believes my regrets
Or takes my demons for fright.

No one hears my cries
No one tastes my despairs
No one feels my sighs
Really, no one cares.

Motherhood

Defective mother
Love in glitch
Numbness and stupor
Biting bitch.

Guilty shadow
Absent smile
Fearful crossbow
Thoughts so vile.

Fainted breath
Heart explodes
Too much depth
Tears exposed.

Tight hold
Pacified
Small hope
Sacrifice.

Today

Today feels like the clouds are heavy,
 The grey of the sky suffocates my soul,
 And the tears of the rain are too hefty,
 For me to climb out of my hole.

Today feels like the wind is pounding,
 Gusts freezing my broken mind,
 And the twirls are thundering and bursting,
 The peace I try desperately to find.

Today feels like a November day,
 The dampness having paralyzed my heart,
 And left my brain in total decay,
 So I give in and embrace my darkest part.

But tomorrow will feel like a sunny beach,
 With hopes tanning all my sorrow,
 And my smile will be a visible speech,
 So my words can sing like a sparrow.

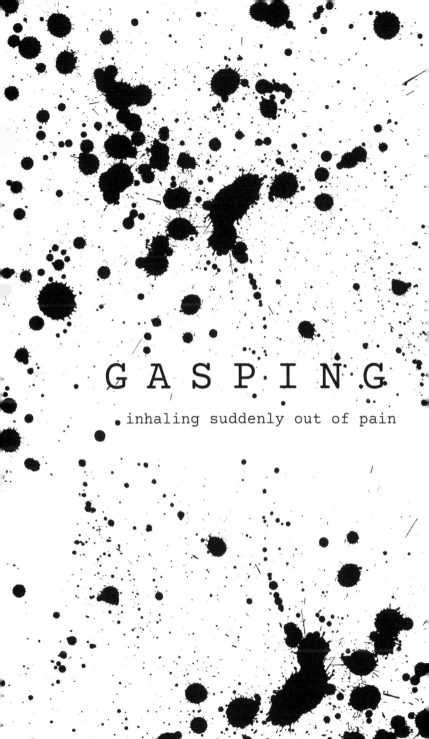

GASPING

inhaling suddenly out of pain

My soul is in heaven
Flying on a cloud
Since I've forgiven
My thoughts for getting loud.
My body is at peace
High on acceptance
Of whom I've ceased
To hate for repentance.
But my heart is in hell
Feeling every flame
Of the love I spell
When I hear your name

Cinnamon

I sparkle hope like cinnamon
On a hot chocolate,
Something that isn't common
And only for a refined palate.

I wake to the wind,
    Whistling at my doubts,
    At my tears, unfeigned
    And my pain being shout.

I doze off to the sea
    Whispering at my fears,
    Everlasting plea
    For me to disappear.

I dream of the mountain
    I thought I couldn't crawl,
    A sorrowful fountain
    Of my deepest downfall.

I live in the dimness
    Of a bottomless well,
    In the wild of the farness
    Where my thoughts unravel.

What Appeases Me

Walking in the snow
A puff of fresh air
A hot cup of tea
A caress in my hair
The warmth of a blanket
Curling in my lair
The sounds of the waves
A few little prayers
And your smile.

Fear of a Woman

Tunnel buzzing
Dimmed light
A stranger
Flee or fight.

Quickened steps
Breath captive
A scream
Afraid to live.

End of night
White ahead
An end
No blood shed.

DEATH

A dead leaf
Frozen by snow
A last kiss
Away you go.

When the shadow of your thoughts becomes too heavy
to bear
Just breathe,
And breathe,
And breathe some more,
Until the light comes in.

STUMBLE

It's not because I have fallen today
That I have failed to recover.

Stained

My doubts are crushing
The life out of me
And all I can do is listen
To them torture me.

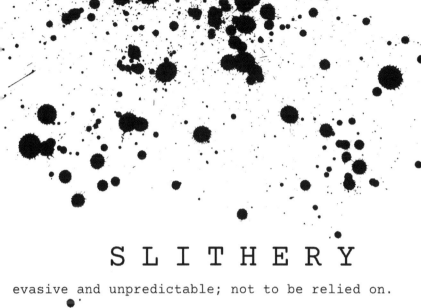

S L I T H E R Y

evasive and unpredictable; not to be relied on.

S.O.S.

I no longer feel safe in my own mind
So tell me, how do I escape?

The monster growls inside of me
    Taking over my sanity.
    I spiral down into my hell,
    Curl back into my fiery shell.
    I scream and shout wordless and mute,
    Jump without my parachute.

My thoughts jostle with all my fears
    And like the sun, darkness sears.
    Boundless loop of crushing doubts,
    I swim toward a lifeless spout,
    And then I crash like waves on shore
    When against myself, I lose the war.

Mind Tricks

Stepping in the snow
I hoped to crush my depression,
But all I did,
Was leave traces of my sorrow.

I love you.
You are enough.
You are bright.
You are brilliant.
You are beautiful.
You deserve love.
I love you.
You are enough.
You are bright.
You are brilliant.
You are beautiful.
You are...

I am a candle in the storm of my thoughts.

I Hate Lavender

There is something
limitless
In the scent of
serenity,
Something making me
relentless
A purple air of
profanity.

Around and around and around
    I row

Infinite catastrophe of possibilities
    I know

Worst case life threatening hazards
    I stow

Shakes of fear and hardened chest
    I grow

Healthy ways to think of us
    I throw

And again in circle
    I go...

Yesterday I promised myself to watch the sun rise on the
water,
But today my heart hurts and my light dims smaller.
So again I let obscurity take over my head,
And stay paralyzed watching night go from my bed.

My Sky

Yellow like the light I try to catch,
Grey like the thoughts clouding my mind,
Blue like the mood I try to unlatch,
White like the peace I'll never find.

Silence
Echos of my pain
Muted
Hope down the drain
Deaf
On my begging knee
Blind
Ignoring my plea
Hurt
A betrayal follows
Blood
For the tears I swallow
Vengeance
Despair sings misery
Death
Alone in victory.

OVERDOSE

an amount of a medicine or drug that is too large.

Tearful Hell
Fell from stars
Depressed veil
Woke my scars
A sudden loss
And bright lies
Burned my cross
And cut all ties
My heart hardened
You screamed respect
And begged pardon
Still a suspect
You cried wolves
And sadness rose
So time dissolved
And suddenly froze.
As I bloomed
In your palm
You presumed
And I crumpled.
I stayed behind
Flew in a swarm
And fought my mind
Wrapped in your storm

Deep down you always knew,
    You could never come to my rescue
    But you let me hope you were shiny and new.

Deep down you always knew,
    I would end up on death avenue
    And you'd boil my heart in a love stew.

Deep down you always knew,
    My darkness was askew
    And your rotting lies were my pew.

Deep down I always knew,
    'Cause you are me and I am you.

Black birds out of my windows
    Invite me to join their murder
    To hold me tight with their claws
    And to let go of what I harbour.

But their words are pure lies,
    I see behind their smiling darts.
    They'll wait for me to desperately die
    And slowly feast on my broken heart.

Daydream

Your love is like a daydream
    Saving me from my inner storms,
    Drops of love coating the seam
    Of the wilderness that inside forms.

Your love is like a daydream
    I must peel myself away,
    'Cos all I hear are the screams
    Of the nightmares of my days.

Your love was like a daydream
    But my monsters ate you alive,
    Nothing was what it seemed
    But without you I can't survive.

The Blue Hour

In the blue hour of our love
I lost myself to dimness
While you walked to the light
And ignored my sadness.

Purple is My Soul

Your fists never bruised
Or made my face bloody
But your words purpled my soul
And made me a nobody.

Scarring my mind forever
And scared it so deeply
That I believed I was an error
Unlovable and greedy.

Your fists never bruised
But your words were deadly
And I found you every excuse
'Cos I loved you sacredly.

Joyful light
Elated song
Small delight
Right or wrong?

Hopeless smile
Sparkled peace
Tearful spile
Darkness ceased.

Winter's lies
Hearts shattered
Saddened eyes
Love mattered.

Spirits laugh
Souls of fool
Epitaph
Sorrowful.

Failure is in my veins
    And your knife is the only way to cure me.

Heartbreak is in my blood
    And your lips are the only way to sooth me.

Insanity is in my mind
    And your love is the only way to appease me.

But revenge is in your heart
    And that's the only way you think of me.

Charming soul
Singing rhymes
Dancing parole
Binding chimes
Lustful smile
Feathered heart
Sullen isle
Nightmare's mart
Aphotic pull
Harmful spell
Mind befouled
Death knell.

Blame

In the darkness, I wake
My soul broken
By the hope I've let in.

Let the wound bleed
  The light of hope
  It's the balm it needs
  For you to cope.

Let the words heal
  Your tearful emptiness
  Let his passion fill
  Your dark nothingness.

Let the lies brush
  Your stubborn black heart
  Listen to his hush
  It's love, for the most part.

INTROSPECTION

a reflective looking inward.

The First Day of Love

Serenity runs in my blood,
It's the first step to self-respect.
It helps me stop the flood
Of the nightfall, I introspect.

My tunnel shines a little brighter
I hope my hell soon will end
And my demons will become smaller
Or at least, become my friends.

Time is said to heal all pains
And as I learn self-compassion
Slowly I bare to stand again
With resilience for companion.

Light enters my deepest scars
Magic balm from up above
And so I thank my lucky stars
For never giving up on love.

Myth of Survival

To kill the monster
Poisoning my mind,
I'll fight back the slaughter
That renders me blind.

I shall listen to my heart
Screaming, I am enough
Silence the imaginary part
Keeping me handcuffed.

I'll take my sword of words
And fight my Cerberus
I'll build a house of cards
And become a murderess.

But most of all I'll whisper
In the name of sorcery
And love myself harder
So my monster becomes puppy.

Me

My heart is a graveyard
    Made of tears and ache
    With prayers that scarred
    Every little heartbreak.

My soul is an arbour
    Blossoming with hope
    That burns with ardour
    All my darkness' grope.

My body is a temple
    To a mental illness
    Protecting the dimples
    Of my emotional distress.

My voice is a weapon
    For whoever hurts
    Who those with peace deaden
    To make pain turn to dirt.

My heart is a graveyard
    That my body abhors
    And my soul is charred
    By my voice screaming orders.

This is me.

CRUSH

Through teas
    and poetry
    I fell in love
    with me

Who I Am

I'm made of volcanoes and earthquakes
Of tears of love and soul aches.
I'm made of Goddess' strength and hope
Of moon's prayers and lover's rope.
I'm made of Heaven and Hell
Of sinful snakes and bright angels.
I'm made of gold and tattoos
Of wolves howling and heart bruise.
I'm made of storm and rhyming words
And I'll fight my mind with song of birds.
I'm made of secrets and spices
And I'll swim ashore my abysses.

I like to shower in the morning dew, it washes off the tears of my darkest night.

Modern-Day Medusa

And when I think of the unknown
My stomach turns into stone.

I am homesick
     Of a time I never knew
     When everything was easier
     When my soul was fresh and new.

I am lovesick
     Of a story that never existed
     When I felt loved and appreciated
     When what I said was never dismissed.

I am seasick
     From the pits of my heart
     When I reminisce my living memories
     All I can do is fall apart.

I am scarsick
     From the depths of my mind
     Because whatever I do to escape
     Can never make me unwind.

I am oversick
     Drugged on my past
     Choking to find air
     But failing, at last.

The Source of The Problem

I am not your prey
    Because you never chased me.

But you are a predator
    Who lingers in my childhood memory.

And if you were alive today
    I would murder you for treachery.

Because I am a survivor
    Of all the times you fondled me.

Queen of Doom

My crown is made of thorns
And my throne of fire
Nonetheless I drown
In the emptiness I desire.

To the scars of childhood
We've been going through
To our little red riding hood
And the wolves we knew.

To the beasts we tamed
Even when we were numb
To the dragons we shamed
And the beauties we've become.

To the villains who thought
They were so good to us
To the princes who were fraught
And the dwarves who fussed.

To the towers of my past
That kept me captive
To the princesses aghast
And the ones attractive.

To the kings who left
Abandoning their thrones
To the committed theft
Of my heart by a crone.

To the witches who raised me
Despite my rotten soul
To the bird who loved me
And my knight who took control.

The ping pong between my personalities
Drives me wild to the point I don't know who to believe
When it comes to loving myself.

I forced my mind to forget
The orchids of my shame
But my heart never met
A flower it could tame.
I drifted into melancholy
Of tulips and memories
Sinking in all my folly
While draped in peonies.
My soul blinded with an old veil
Believed the lilies of the valley
And got poisoned with the tale
Of their nectar I sipped gladly.
Laid down on a path of roses
I flew like birds of paradise
And with my pocket full of posies
Fell into the garden of vice.
There I played with carnations
While Lady's Mantles clustered the stars
And my bleeding heart found salvation
In every petal it called scars.
So I dried the magical tears
And when the lilac turned lavender
I fought all of my fears
And in a swirl of daisies, surrendered.

PASSING

carried out quickly and lightly.

SURRENDER

Racing heart
Short breath
Churning stomach
Thoughts of death.

Warden tears
Clenched jaw
Sudden fear
Overdraw.

Cold hands
Deep fatigue
Satan's plans
Lives concede.

—-

I was holding on
    By a thread to life
    Swimming like a swan
    On the blade of a knife.

I was hoping for more
    For a little attention
    Fighting a cold war
    Of all rejection.

I was praying for peace
    To end my melancholy
    Crying for all to cease
    Before madness takes me.

I just had to let go
    To slowly slice my wrist
    But then I heard a crow
    And decided to exist.

Hiding
Lying
Crying
Pretending
Smiling
Sleeping
Hurting
Rotting
Waiting
To be free.

CHECK MATE

Sometimes all I can do

　　　　　　　Is let the demons win

Slumber of darkness
    Slither of hope
    Path of sadness
    Love kaleidoscope.

Ocean of pain
    Clouds of sunshine
    Feelings all drain
    Spirits of wine.

Tears of depression
    Smile so heavy
    Silent procession
    Grief confetti.

Every night I wish upon a star
To close my eyes and au revoir.

Every morning I thank the sleeping moon,
For not having taken me so soon.

But it's the sun that saves my life,
Always shining in time of strife.

Let me become ashes,
    Let me disappear
    Wipe my eyelashes
    Dry each of my tears.

Let me burn in grief
    Let me quiet the fight
    Murder in me the thief
    Who stole all my light.

Let me ignite the stake
    Let me feel the heat,
    Silence all the ache
    Of my soul incomplete.

Let me become ashes,
    Let me disappear,
    As the red sun flashes
    Make my blooded heart smear.

Grey screams echo

        The silence in my mind

                I plea for it to end.

INNOCENCE

Black snow swirls
Upon my face
Evil pearls
Fragile lace.

Numbness laughs
At my expense
Liquor draughts
No sixth sense.

Deep doldrums
Swallow me
Life's old hymns
Ultimate plea.

Voiceless songs
Grisly tango
To death belongs
My last flambeau.

IF

If I disappear
  Listen to the sea

If I disappear
  It will tell you where I'll be.

If I disappear
  You'll have to promise me

If I disappear
  You won't come looking for me.

If I disappear
  Please set me free

If I disappear
  What will be will be.

I am a prisoner of my own mind
Rancorously, I threw away the key.
My only hope is for my tormentor to unwind
So I can slice my bonds and die free.

I feel disconnected, always simply alone.
    I feel no one understands the gloom I've shown.

I feel lost forever, like an orphan of my own thoughts.
    I feel unlovable, bearing my own cross.

I feel prettier, when my monster grows.
    I feel my smile can hide all my sorrows.

I feel like you see me, but you're blind to my pain.
    I feel like I love you and misery all the same.

I feel you will hate me, for the distress I'll cause you.
    I feel so empty when my heart is blue.

I feel tired of living, a life that is not real.
    But I know I should be happy, because at least,

I feel.

RESURGENCE

a rising again into life, activity, or prominence.

Shhhh

Hear the voices,
    Shush the smiles
    and hurt through your words

Can you hear the tears of the butterfly?
    It guides their wings far from home.
    And once drenched they slowly die
    Like the voices in the catacombs.

Can you hear the sigh of the trees?
    They scream the loss of the wind.
    Falling apart on their knees
    Praying for their love to get twinned.

Can you hear the whisper of the waves?
    They call my name night and day.
    Preparing my solstice grave,
    For when I'll be ready to play.

Can you hear the silence of nature?
    Waiting for you to forgive,
    All of the demoniac creatures
    Who scared you to sing and live.

The North Star never stopped shinning
   But the darkness has rendered me blind

SUFFOCATE

Panic settles on my throat
Choking me silent
And the breath I need to calm my thoughts
Morphing my death, unspeakably violent.

When will they notice...
    My smile hides my demons
    And their grip on my feelings.

When will they notice...
    I don't like to be alone
    But can't figure out, my own way home.

When will they notice...
    My whispers are screams
    And nothing is like it really seems.

When will they notice...
    My pain daily grows
    And coats my mind like fresh snow.

When will they notice...
    I'm not who I'm supposed to be
    But all I do, is flee...

Time Travel

I want to go back
To a time
When I could smile
And feel it in my blood.

I was made of dirt,
Angel of the kingdom below
Accustomed to hurt
But hidden from crossbow.
I had broken wings
And scars from sturdy chains
Was at the mercy of kings
Who fed on my veins.
I prayed to the witches
For freedom and peace
But it was the goddesses
Who heard all my pleas.
They took me apart
Made me a fiend
Removed my stung heart
And programmed me to sin.
Then the hunter came
So, I ran to the woods
He tried to take his claim
But with my heart went my good.
And I bit and I fought
Until my last feather
And never got caught
By this bird collector.
I wandered exhausted
Until the star appeared
Waited to be frosted
For my guilt to be cleared
But there is no absolution
For angels who kill men

Only retribution
And capture once again.
My feather turned black
As well as my soul
There was no turning back
I had no control.
I heard the Devil laugh
As I returned to mud
All this was his craft
My hell and his blood.

Wind whistle
Snowfall
Still winter
Montreal.

Hurtful steps
Creepy sounds
Dirty sex
Salt on wounds.

Harmless fling
Burning scars
Broken ring
Shooting star.

No voices
Silent heart
Hard choices
Fall apart.

Distant tear
Erased bind
Muted fears
Mind unkind

There is a universe
Where happiness reaches my heart
I wish I were there.

I still feel you
     And your slimy body
     Your cold fingers
     Groping little me
     Your open pants
     Me on your laps
     Army of ants
     Felt in your traps

I still see you
     And feel betrayed
     Everyone knew
     And silent stayed
     They said enough
     After a while
     My screams handcuffed
     I simply smiled

I still smell you
     And your stench kisses
     Your harsh breath
     Disgust blisses
     The horrors stay
     In my nightmares
     I can't slay
     All my despair

I still hear you
     And your honeyed voice
     Your compliments

Your tongue's noise
I hurt in vain
Now that you're dead
I feel insane
My mind bloodshed

SALVATION

liberation from ignorance or illusion.

Whispered Truce

Counting your blessings
On the tips of your fingers
Murmur your depression
Like a dirty prayer.

It's easy to forget
How much one is loved
While choking on threats
Under sadness' gloves.

Focus on the light
Let it bathe your wounds
Hold yourself tight
Call back your howling hounds.

Accept your truce
That comes with shivers
Push away your self-abuse
And start smiling in the mirror.

A pinch of bravery to survive emotional distress
    A spoonful of resilience to disobey a sick mind
    A cup of patience to word the sadness
    And ounces of boldness, to oneself be kind.

Letter to Self

I understand you're working on old wounds
And I hope you find answers
To the malaise you always confound
With what life has given you as circumstances.

I know you hurt from dusk to dawn.
I hear your cries and confessions,
Bear in mind you're a magnificent swan
That has blossomed despite rejection.

Remember no child is born able to walk,
Be patient and learn to love yourself
And show your demons who like to stalk
That you are the master of your own self.

Today I feel like the clouds,
 Light but sliding across my scars
 As I stand tall and proud
 At the altar of my wars.

Today I feel like a petal
 Fragile and exquisite
 But most of it indispensable
 To the flower I exhibit.

Today I feel like the ocean
 And every sea on earth
 Quiet and still of emotions
 That have been shaking my worth.

Today I feel like the wind
 Blowing the air high above
 As I whisper in my dream
 That it's with me whom I'm in love.

MIRROR, MIRROR

We've heard the story of Narcissus so many times,
    That we fear to love
    whom we see in the mirror.

Crystals, sage and other witchery
Lead the way of my recovery.
Prayers, spells and incantation
Calm the waves of my depression.
But it's only when I think of you,
that I smile.
Only when I think of you,
That my pain
Is versatile

Peace

Calm is the lake
Surrounding my heart
But it's the skies in my mind
That spit fires into my doubts
And transform a peaceful sunrise
Into a Hell for my soul

Mend your heart
Cry all night
Rise apart
Flee or fight

Take a breath
One small step
Avoid death
Thank you next

Close your eyes
Hold your foul
Stop the lies
Heal your soul

Hope
in the palm of my hand
Dancing like swirling snow
Crushed
when I tried to stand
I never liked winterland.

B A L A N C E

mental and emotional steadiness.

In the shortest days of my life,
Hope resurges from their ashes

Like the sun rebirths in the darkness
Like a Phoenix revives in nothingness
Like love renews in emptiness.

Gifts, love, time, care
I gave too much
To too many people
And lost myself to generosity
To hide my avarice of words.

And then I learned to love myself
Through your eyes
And all the gifts, love, time and care I gave
Became reasons to arise instead than to despise
Myself.

My scars are a compass
Pointing toward my pains.
Please handle with care.

As Elsa Says

All I had to do was let it go
But I was too busy holding onto my ghostly past
To find peace

I tried to slice my wrists with my sharp teeth
But my self-loathing wasn't enough to destroy me
So I learned how to breathe
And it's my self-love that set me free.

O.V.E.R

Overjoyed
Overhyped
Overwhelmed
Overgrown

Overloved
Overlooked
Overflown
Over-owned

Over-fought
Over Me
Over who I assumed I'll be

Overthought
Over you
Over what I was meant to be.

FRIENDSHIP

A sip of courage
    A dance under the stars
    The chirping of birds
    Quiet my inner scars

The silence of life
    The screams of my brain
    A rumble in the sky
    Revive all my pain

Before me I have the choice
    To come back to who I was
    Or reinvent my voice
    And embrace my new flaws

'Cos Mental Health is a war
    A fight against oneself
    A take down with a mirror
    Who craves blood and farewell

So hold my hand or leave
    But decide wisely
    If you're here to conceive
    I won't let you destroy me

Christmas light
    Food delight
    Presents night
    Not a fight.

Silent pain
    Voice contained
    Candy Canes
    Love in vain.

Bright eyes
    No more lies
    New allies
    Gloom dies.

Dried weep
    Soft sleep
    Faith leap
    Loving deep.

Gentle grin
    Repent sin
    Fatal spin
    Peace within.

FEAR ME NOT

I feared so much and so many
That I didn't realize the only
Thing I was really scared of
Was my duplicity.

I don't recognize myself anymore
Because who I used to be
Loved darkness more than anything
But who I became
Loves nothing more than herself

What a change this is...

The Road Back to Myself

I followed the wrong path
    Took some muddy tearful detours
    Tripped on a soulless lath
    And ended up on all fours

I fell into a hole
    Held onto some climbing lies
    Forgot to feed my soul
    And saw myself slowly die

Lastly I found a map
    But had a hard time reading it
    Because I was just scraps
    Of my worst mental wit

Suddenly I understood
    There was no road back to me
    I wasn't who I should
    Life had changed me.

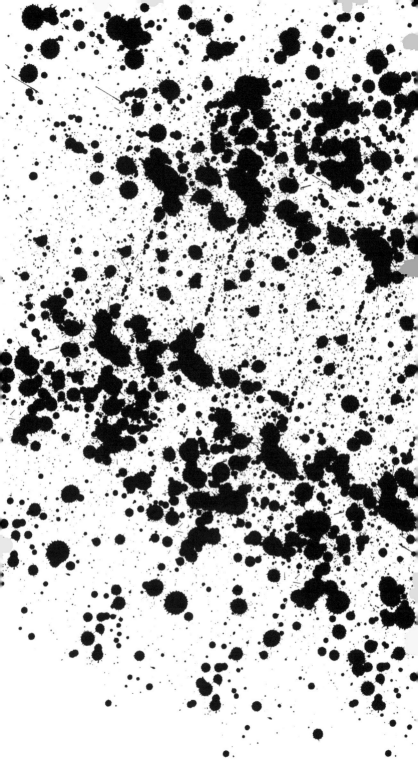

RELAPSE

a recurrence of symptoms of a disease
after a period of improvement.

Setback

I thought I was healed
But one knock on the door of darkness
Reminded me my fiends weren't sealed

_____

For every smile I gave in the light of day
I shed a tear in the shadow of night.

Regret
Rebirth
Regrowth
Revamp
Reward
Relief
Remake
Recon
Rebel
Re-al
Re-st
R-end

Maybe I like nightfall too much to heal

———

Show me your hell,
    And I'll show you my spring.

Show me your dreams,
    And I'll show you my wings.

Show me your smile,
    And I'll show you my flags.

Show me your sleet,
    And I'll show you my slags.

Show me your thorns,
    And I'll show you my vines.

Show me all yours,
    And I'll hide from you mine.

Mermaid

My madness is a siren
Chanting its hypnosis
And its darkness has me feeding
My demonic psychosis.

It isn't sadness that weighs on my soul
But the emptiness you left behind
When you destroyed my last glimmer of hope.

BIASED

My life has no colour
Black and white is my sight
Even the flowers
Budding from the light

I don't want to live
But I don't want to die
It takes too much strive
To plan for the skies

I'm drowning in grey
While others breathe in pink
So I stand at bay
Of people who don't sink

I lost who I am
Total disconnection
Waiting to be shammed
Out of depression

I've fallen in love with the dark side of me
Let the crow eat my dove and morph me to fury
As I joined their murder, I still flew alone
'Cos self-love is harder when your wings weight your bones.
But with heights and regrets always come perspectives
I might love and forget, but will never forgive.

THE DRAGONFLY

The whispers of the red dragonfly
    Woke the terrors of our love,
    And while the snow melts on our hearts
    Tainted is the peace I dreamt of.

As your sunshine disappears
    Grey are the days of my gloom
    And while I feed my depression
    I hear them laugh across the room.

They were waiting for the full moon
    To feast on all of my mistakes
    And while I tripped on happiness
    They lit the fire on their stakes.

Now the dragonfly dances
    To the beat of the demons' howl
    And while beautifully, I rot
    I suck on darkness and fall.

People say I look good
When I am too skinny
People say I look peaceful
When I'm not even happy
People judge my actions
Instead of watching their own
People blame my passion
Instead of leaving me alone
People get hurt in their ego
Because I've told them some truth
People act like placebo
Holding on to their youth
People don't see I'm pretending
Even if they are masters at it
But they are the first offended
And end friendships or call it quits
People walk in and out
Taking everything I can offer
And don't care to see me without
The smile I wear while I suffer.

Unworthiness

Through the cracks of my scars
The whispers became louder
So I listened, to them

They sang lies I believed
About my worst nightmare
So I blindly, joined them

Their cruelty stabbed my heart
With mockery and laughter
But nonetheless I, helped them

In choking my sanity
To kill all that mattered
And chanting my requiem, with them

My eyes are filled with sand
Now that they are out of tears
As if the Sahara Desert had numbed my feelings.
I'm just waiting for the storm to pass.

The Last Breath

I swam in the abysses of my sins
And drowned in the well of my pain
But with one breath
I found force in my chagrin
And rebirthed from the depths of my strain

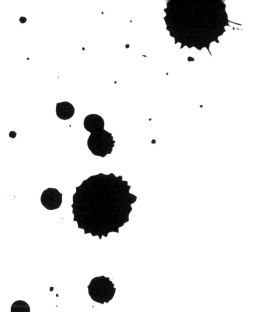

H E A L I N G

to restore to original purity or integrity.

It's when you get tired of acting
When the smile and mask fall
That your healing can finally begin.

I love the sun,
    Hellfire in the skies of all dreams
    Brightest stars burning of all gleam
    Gods power of all the self esteem.

But it has nothing on the moon,
    Patiently waiting for its turn to shine
    Without ever burning inside
    But still majestic and divine.

Both are here to guide me
    But it's in your rainbow that I find the strength
    To flee.

THERAPY

It takes a lot of courage to say out loud
Things you've been whispering to yourself
So know that whatever you feel, I'm proud
Of you for voicing all the pain you withheld

My life upside down
Drowning in a water glass
Mind flowers bloom wild.

Goodbye to my Evil Twin

Building my altar,
I climb out of hell
Alone with my monsters
Attached to my barbell.

Carrying my weight
And my melancholy
I accept my mistake
And refuse your folly.

If I was a victim
It was only from your actions,
Your words were twisted,
And brought me to depression.

Now a survivor,
I deploy all my strength,
Killing my impostor,
For peace to come at length.

No Regrets

I lost myself to the deepest darkness
And found myself on the path of self-love and self-kindness.

So tell me, how can I regret having wanted to die?

VICTORY

Cold winds caress my face
Winter cheers for my gloom
Nevertheless I smile.

LAST WORDS TO MY BULLY

————

I fell in love with whom I was
    In the darkness
    Of time

I worked on being gentle with myself
    In the ugliness
    Of life

I killed my fears and my worries
    In the strangeness
    Of mind

I healed and became someone else
    In the brightness
    Of night

But it's in the beauty of day
    That I sauntered
    Away

From you

I learned to breathe when I choked on words
    When my mind fogged up with my demons
    When gloom took over the sound of birds
    And I seemed to be stuck in despair season.

I learned to breathe when I closed my heart
    When I became blind to the beauty around
    When I slowly teared myself apart
    And the decay in my soul made me drowned.

I learned to breathe before it was too late
    When I knew this life was my last chance
    When the broken wings became a weight
    I needed to remove to properly dance.

I learned to breathe like others learned to walk
    One step at the time, with a lot of stumbles
    With my first gasp, I learned to talk,
    And saw the light in my struggles.

What is the meaning of love
But to become at peace with oneself ?

Rooted

My roots were tangled in traumas of my childhood
So I took a comb and patiently worked my way through
It hurt like a bitch but made me good,
To heal the wounds of how I grew.

I wish I could tell you,
I'm healed from my past
But I prefer to eschew
Lies that will last.

I'm a work in progress
Riding waves of melancholy,
Cinnamon to the distress
I dance in my folly.

I need a few more steps,
Some more doses of patience
I've lost friends and respect
In this game of tolerance.

Through my mental hell,
I avoided all sparks
I walked on eggshells
And lost my landmarks.

I've built myself again
From my self-destruction
But had to abstain,
From some interactions.

To all those who stayed
You showed me what love was
And helped me mislay
The voices I couldn't pause.

I'm on the rollercoaster
Of what we call life
And it might not be closure,
But for the moment, I smile.

Exhale

In the end I was just a girl,
Broken beyond repair,
Patched up by years of lies,
Who faked every smile
To be sure she was loved.

But now I'm a woman,
Built from invisible moans
Howled in muteness
On the shoulder of despair,
Embracing my renewal.

END OF STORY

I was trapped in a psychological twilight zone and I hurt so much I wanted to die.

It came upon me slowly, like a veil I was blind to and took over every one of my thoughts. I've made mistakes, become the villain of some stories and the victim of others. I've cried, stared into space, thought I would never feel better, relapsed, laughed, faked life, love, motherhood. I've hurt and lost friends in the process of losing myself, but I also found new ones and rekindled with old ones who could support me. I discovered a new love for nature and dove into art and poetry.

I didn't recognize myself anymore, went to therapy and realized it was time to deal with some heavy traumas.

The universe threw some huge obstacles in my way, the kind of things no parents want to deal with... but I learned to hold on to peace in the chaos surrounding me, I learned to embrace boredom and push away anyone trying to hold on to the old me. And then... when it was time to be myself again, I had changed so much I needed to learn who I was.

I hope this collection of poems shows you hope in the despair you or a loved one is going through. I am not healed, I am a work in progress, but I am on the right path of becoming who I was meant to be.

Thank you to everyone who was part of this journey. The ones who stayed and the ones who left. You all helped me transform my pain into art and for this I will be eternally grateful.

I leave you with these words from Leonard Cohen.

"A cry of pain in itself is just that. It can affect you or you can turn away from it. But a piece of work that treats the experience that produced the cry of pain is a different matter altogether. The cry is transformed, alchemised, by the work by a certain objectivity that doesn't surrender the emotion but gives it form. That's the difference between life and art."

Take care of yourself,
Gabrielle

Follow me on Instagram (AuthorGabrielleG) or Facebook (GabrielleGPoetry) for daily (or almost daily) poetry.

ABOUT THE AUTHOR

Gabrielle G will do anything for a hot cup of tea, still celebrates her half birthdays and feels everyone has an inner temptuous voice.

Born in France and having lived in Switzerland, Gabrielle currently resides in Montreal with her husband, three teenagers and a moody cat.

After spending years contemplating a career in writing, she finally jumped off the deep end and took the plunge into the literary world. Writing consumed her and she independently published her work.

Gabrielle's style is fiercely raw and driven by pure emotion. Her stories and poetry leave you out of breath, yearning for more, while at the same time wiping away tears.

Visit www.authorgabrielleg.com for more details

Printed in Great Britain
by Amazon

77196646R00102